I am 3318052 Private John Savage previously of 'C' Company which is part of the 5th Battalion Highland Light Infantry. The battalion is part of the 157 Brigade and we are all members of the 52nd Lowland Division.

This is the true account of what took place in France during a few days in June of 1940. What little information there is about those days is flawed and my account gives the true version of events.

Contact
johnsavage@hotmail.co.uk

Also by John Savage

Ye Olde Antique Shoppe

~

The Untold Story
of the
52nd Lowland Division in
France during days in June of 1940.

An extract from the book

Ye Olde Antique Shoppe

By

John Savage

Glenn G. Morrison
1189 Dover Ave.
Columbus, OH. 43212
614-291-8147

First published in Great Britain in July 2009
Reprinted September 2009
This print April 2013

The author has given his permission for a short extract of
this book to be reprinted on the BBC web site
ww2peopleswar.

www.scotsatwar.org.uk/veteransreminiscences/jsavage.htm

Printed in the USA

Photo from original & copyright of the author.

Manuscript proof read & typed by
D. Smith and K. Smith.
Layout by C & W Savage.

Email: johnsavage@hotmail.co.uk
www.52ndlowlanddivision.co.uk

To My Wife Mary
With Love

Preface

'The Ye Olde Antique Shoppe' is a book I wrote in 1992. It is in longhand. It was written for family purposes only.

So what you are about to read now, is an extract from the above book slightly more updated than the original. The reason for this is that someone has been living a lie for many years, yes over sixty years. That of course is only the truth if the same said someone is alive today. He could have passed away many years ago, I don't know. If he is dead the truth will not hurt him now and that is what I am trying to achieve, the truth, and why this person took the credit for something I did in France in June of 1940.

I only found this out in 1999 when I was advised by Dr Diane Henderson, Research Director for the Scots at War Trust. She advised me to read a book which was titled 'Mountain and Flood' by G. Blake, published in Glasgow in 1950. This I did and when I read a paragraph on page 27 of that book I was annoyed. So this is my story.

Chapter 1

We all know that something is brewing. The battalion has moved so many times in so few weeks. We left the Long Burton area and moved to the army camp in Tidworth Park and from there to Delvilla Barracks in Cove, Hampshire.

We are still moving; we are on the march to Farnborough railway station. We do know that when we board the train our destination is Southampton, that is all we have been told. Some of the lads keep saying to me.

'You must know where we are going, you are in Company HQ and you are the CO`s orderly.'

Yes I am the CO's orderly; I am 3318052 Private J. Savage. Major Channer is my boss and he does not give away many secrets, in fact he does not give away any. He is in command of 'C' Company which is part of the 5th Battalion Highland Light Infantry. The battalion is part of the 157 Brigade and we are all members of the 52nd Lowland Division.

We have arrived at Southampton and we are now in the dock area. It looks like we are going on a cruise. It must be a very short cruise as we have not been inoculated, nor have we been issued with any tropical kit so we are not going to the Middle East. Some troops are already aboard ship so we march up the gangway and take our place in the area marked `C` Company. The ship left its berth; there were a few last farewells from the uniformed personnel and the dock workers   "Good luck lads!" followed by a few waves of their hands.   No wives or sweethearts, no last minute hugs, no goodbye kisses, it was all so 'hush hush'. We were on the ship and we could not get off.

It is now 15:00 hours on the 7th June 1940. We are now in our position in the convoy and the anchor has been dropped. We sail at 23:00 hours under the cover of darkness. The engine has started up, the ship is on the move and you can feel the vibration as she gathers speed. We have now been told our destination, it took most of us by surprise, also scared the living daylights out of us. We have been told that the Germans have broken through the French/Belgian border and are now pushing up through northern France. The orders and our objective are to get as near to Paris as possible, get in a defensive position and wait for the Germans to attack.

Four days ago hundreds of thousands of British, French and Belgian troops had been evacuated from the beaches of Dunkirk. King

Leopold III has surrendered. Everyone knows that France is on the verge of collapse so it looks very much like we have been given a one way ticket.

We have been told that we will land at Cherbourg. Transport will be available to take us near to our defensive positions; we may even reach Paris before the Germans do. It seems sheer madness to send two divisions to Paris at a time like this.

We were off the coast of France the following morning, no German aircraft overhead. We had to wait our turn before we could berth so it was 13:00 hours on the 8th June, a beautiful afternoon, as we marched down the gangway of the ship and our feet touched French soil. Was this our final destination? What had we to look forward to? A German prisoner of war camp or perhaps a six foot hole in the French soil?

We had been issued with fifty rounds of ammunition, one bandolier and two hand grenades which we had to sign for; you have to sign for everything you receive, only this time you don't have to hand them back.

We assembled in the dock area, each Company a group on their own, waiting for the order to move. This takes time, from the French

HQ to our Divisional HQ then to Brigade HQ, from there to Battalion HQ. From Battalion HQ to Co. HQ and when the time was right, the Co. would inform the platoon sergeants, the platoon sergeants would shout.

'Right lads, on your feet, get ready to move.'

As we marched out of the harbour area and into the streets of Cherbourg, small boys were cheering, girls were waving and kissing some of the lads, but the older men and women of Cherbourg were telling us to go home. They were shouting,

'la boche la boche is coming, go home, go home.'

They knew the Germans were coming, so did we, but we could not go home, we had a job to do, so we were going up to meet them, perhaps delay their advance so that the French might carry the fighting on for a few more weeks. This would give Britain a few more weeks to prepare for a German invasion.

Most of us knew that this mission was bound to fail, it was suicidal and on such a lovely day; so we shall have to make the best of it, after all you can only die once. Treat it as just another manoeuvre, only this time the enemy are real and so are the bullets and the odds against us must be well over 1000/1.

We had only been marching for about twenty minutes when we were given the order to halt. We were well clear of the harbour area so if 'Jerry' decided to bomb, we would not be the target. The officers were studying one of the maps and the lads were sitting on the grass verge by the side of the road. This was the first time any of us would be taking part in a real battle, a battle we knew we could not win.

The feeling amongst us was tense, no one was expressing an opinion of what lay ahead because no one knew.

We are on the move again, we are not in enemy territory at the moment but we are in a hostile environment so we are no longer marching in columns of three, the order of march is, scouts up in front then the CO and myself, then the IO (Intelligence Officer) and the CSM which is the Company Sergeant Major, then the platoons section by section on both sides of the road with three yards between each man.

Our first stop will be St. Pierre Eglise, about twenty kilometres from our starting point, on the main coast road. We are moving away from Cherbourg in a westerly direction when we reach our chosen destination. It turned out to be a large chateau, much larger than most of our country houses. The officers might be very lucky; other ranks will have to bivouac in the grounds surrounding the chateau. Most of us managed to get a few hours sleep, we did a lot of talking amongst ourselves, we also had to keep an eye on the sky for German paratroopers. There was quite a bit of aircraft noise during the night, this did not affect us in any way. The night passed very slowly and we were glad when the early morning light appeared. I can't remember what the QMS (Quarter Master Sergeant) dished up for breakfast, maybe we didn't have any.

It was now 06:00 hours on the 9th June. Within the hour the MT (Motor Transport) had arrived. We had been allocated four covered-in trucks. We also had the QMS truck. Before we boarded the transport we were ordered to clean up our area. There is a war on. Before we take part in it we have to pick up all the discarded rubbish, empty cigarette packets and a number of empty wine bottles; the French had been very generous to us whilst on the march.

We board the transport and move off. The going was very slow; the roads are full of refuges that had all manner of transport, mostly farm vehicles. We have covered about three hundred kilometres, nearly two hundred miles.

The convoy stopped when a dispatch rider halted the leading truck and gave our CO a message, perhaps a new set of orders because the CO got out of the truck and onto the back of the dispatch riders bike. He was going to Battalion HQ.

We were allowed out of the trucks. We had been given rations on the boat, biscuits, the hard type, a packet would last you all day and perhaps break your two front teeth. I still had mine; it was just as well, ten yards from where we stopped was a bakers shop. He sold us French bread and fancy cakes. Next door to the bakers was a small grocery shop. We bought some bottles of lager.

We were all on the transport when the CO arrived back. He came back the same way as he had gone, on the back of a dispatch riders bike. It was not very long before our convoy of five trucks moved off again. We had only been going for about twenty minutes; the convoy had stopped to take on petrol. We had quite a number of stops; nobody seemed to know why as all we had been told was that we were heading for the Le Mans area.

We were moving much faster now as the flow of refugees had gone down to a trickle. Most of them were pushing hand carts, even prams. It was late in the evening when the convoy came to a stop. We had come off a major road and onto a secondary road. We stopped at a place called Maresche. We had only covered another ninety or a hundred miles and we had not seen one angry German during our travels.

This was to be our stopping place for the night. Only 'C' Company was in this area, we had no billets so it was to be another night under the stars. We were in another wooded area; this also helped to camouflage the transport. We had been told that there were no German troops in the vicinity. The nearby crossroad had been manned and the sentries told to look out for the troop carrying vehicles, also German paratroopers. They were also warned not to shoot at any of our French allies.

The QM Sergeant had a meal ready for us by midnight. He had plenty of help because HQ staff was not doing sentry duty at the moment. The meal consisted of some kind of stew, bits of dumpling and boiled potatoes with rice to follow and plenty of tea and French bread. The tea was also available all night.

On the morning of the 10th June we were told that we were now under the command of The French Army and were awaiting further orders. We stayed at Maresche for two full days and one night; lucky the weather was warm and dry as we were still sleeping under the starry sky.

It was on the night of June 11th we were told to be ready to move at 06:00 hours the following morning. Destination somewhere in the area of Conches, this was to be our final position. We boarded the transport at the stated time. Whilst en route the orders were changed once again because of the rapid German advance. It makes our move to the intended area impossible. You cannot defend an area that is already occupied by the enemy, so we bypassed Conches and travelled further in a south westerly direction. Our new position is to be the railway line between Basque and Evreux. This will only be a stopping off place, another night under the stars. We had travelled about sixty kilometres today, 12th June.

We had still not seen hide nor hair of the German army, lots of shell fire overhead and in the distance fires could be seen blazing. None of this affected us in any way.

Our Company, that is `C` Company, were rather lucky regarding our overnight position. We had been put in reserve, the other Companies were now ahead of us, we were on the banks of a river and our bivouac was in the orchard. The apples were ripe, we also had a potato field nearby, so along with our dry rations we had roasted potatoes.

This is our fifth day in France it is now 18:00 hours on 12th June. The QMS has just come back from BN HQ. He has unloaded from his wagon the necessary items for the brewing of tea. He also unloaded one gents bicycle. It was not brand new; I had used it often on manoeuvres when Major Atkins was in charge of 'C' Company. We got on very well as I had met his wife and family a few times while in Perth Barracks. I was his runner when we did commando training on the Isle of Mull. The last I heard of Major Aitkins was when he went on leave early in May, given an extended leave and then was transferred to a Highland Division.

I don't know Major Channer very well; he has only been with the Company these last two weeks. I have only spoken to him on two or three occasions whilst on office duties. He seems to know what he is doing so we may get on alright. When I was given the cycle I was also given the map case and the torch, the CO kept the binoculars, so I got to know the route we had taken and the names of some of the French villages. We stayed in our position most of the day and had bathed in the river, washed some of our clothing, got a bit of the sun and late in the evening we chose where we were going to sleep; were told not to sleep in any of the trucks. The officers came round during the hours of darkness and spoke to those who were still awake. We spent most of the night talking, smoking and drinking tea. In the morning, 13th June, I found myself in charge of transport, one gents cycle, the motor transport had gone; even the Quarter Masters truck had disappeared. I had a good look at the map of the area we were in, also the other five maps that were in the case. The CO had circled some of the towns and villages whilst travelling in the MT so it was easy to see the way we had arrived at this spot.

At the moment 'C' Company is still in reserve in the outskirts of a village known as Les Buisson. Battalion HQ is in the village, 'A' Company in Ferriere near to Clocher area and 'B' Company is in Portes. 'A' and 'B' Co's are digging in, this is their final position.

At 11:00 hours Major Channer told junior officers and NCO that 'C' Company will advance to Faverolles-la-Champagne about eight kilometres away. Would this be the point of no return? We had been told on previous occasions that there would be no surrender, when the time came it would be a last man, last bullet situation.

Our task was to delay the German advance for as long as possible.

Chapter 2

We were now ready to move. We came out of the shady orchard and into blazing sunshine. This time we left behind all the empty cigarette packets, lumps of stale bread, half eaten apples and the ashes from the fires we had lit.

The order of march was as follows: two scouts ahead, two more well behind, then came HQ then CO and the Sergeant Major, then myself pushing the cycle. Then came the rest of 'C' Company on both sides of the road about three yards between each man. We marched out of the orchard and over the river bridge. We were on our way to our defensive position somewhere in the area of Faverolles-la-Campagne. We had the road to ourselves; the other Companies may have used the same road at different times. We passed by Battalion's Headquarters and we were now leaving Les Buisson. They were remaining for the time being. I only used the cycle a few times when the CO wanted the scouts to halt and when he wanted to speak to other officers.

We had covered about five miles when the CO called a halt. We came off the road and onto a very rough lane. It had a high hedge, this was on the right hand side of the lane and it also had a ditch about four feet deep. After about a mile we turned right into a farm area, the Company was halted. A farmer and a female companion, who could have been his wife, were very distraught and one of our officers who spoke a bit of French was trying to console them. It seems they were ready to leave the area, they had a tractor with bits of luggage already on it but they wanted us to move on. They knew there was a war going on but they did not want it in their back garden. They finally moved on when they realised this was our final stopping place.

The entrance to the farm was about twenty feet wide. On the right hand side was a very large barn and nearby was a very big oak tree. The front of the farm house could be seen from the lane. About fifty yards separated the barn from the farmhouse. It was in this area that most of the lads were taking it easy, some lay down, some sat and smoked, others were eating bits of French bread and the officers were having a confab.

I left the cycle leaning against the old oak tree. This was now the time to take precautions as the enemy were somewhere in front of us. We were in a very precarious situation.

The proper use of cover could save your life so at the moment the old oak tree separated me from the possible snipers. The farmhouse was completely surrounded by a three foot high black and white fence.

I believe the fence protected the farmer's wife's vegetable patch and flower garden from any stray animals. At the moment none could be seen.

The farmhouse and the surrounding area were very tranquil. Was this the calm before the storm? The view from the rear of the farmhouse, a large field, it seems to stretch for miles in both easterly and westerly directions. Whatever crop that had been grown there had been cut and removed, so now the whole field was covered in stubble two of three inches high, no trees; no cover of any kind that the Germans could use if and when they decided to attack. If they made a frontal attack they would have to come out of a dense wood. This was about three or four hundred yards from the farmhouse.

The CO's meeting came to an end. The Platoon Officers now knew what was required of them so Platoon Sergeants started shouting.

'On your feet 7 Platoon, 9 Platoon on your feet, 8 Platoon fall in.'

Company HQ was staying in the farm area.

7 Platoon left the farm area and made a right turn. They would take up a position half a mile further down the lane. They would be very near to the village of Faverolles-la-Campagne. 8 Platoon was in reserve on the other side of the lane. 9 Platoon turned left from the farm and went back the way we had come. They had to find a suitable position half a mile to the right of HQ. I knew the exact positions of 7 and 9 Platoons as I had been sent to them on a number of occasions. They had both made good use of the ready made ditch. 8 Platoon could be seen from the lane, they did not have to dig trenches.

It is now 13:00 hours on 13th June, unlucky for some. Sergeant Major Breame has marked out the positions where the trenches will be dug. It will be two men to a trench. Three trenches were dug each side of the farmhouse, this side of the fence and two more outside the farm area. We kept the fence in front of us upright, removed a few of the railings so that we had all round vision and we flattened the rest of the fences.

'C' Company were in position, we were ready to take on the might of the German Army. During our travel by transport we had not seen hide nor hair of 'A' or 'B' Companies. I knew by the map that there was a four mile gap between Companies. It might as well have been a hundred mile gap as each Company had to fight their own battles. No heavy artillery, no British tanks, the battalion has four Bren carriers; 'C' Company had not been given the use of any of them.

The trenches had all been dug four foot deep. They had to be manned at all times. Because of the blazing sunshine and stifling heat it was decided each man would do one hour in the trenches during daylight hours and during the hours of darkness it would be two on four off. Both windows at the rear of the farmhouse had the panes of glass removed and Bren guns put in position. Those not on duties had the use of the barn. At the first sign of trouble all trenches had to be occupied. Additional hand grenades and rifle ammunition were within easy reach of the trenches.

During our travels the days had seemed very long. Most of the lads had been fed up, bored with the journey, not knowing what they had to do or what was expected of them. First we had left Cherbourg, travelled in a westerly direction, retraced our steps through Cherbourg again, then the coast road to the east, then north to the Le Mans area, then across France again to Faverolles-la-Campagne. We arrived here about

13:00 hours. It is now 15:00 hours, the trenches have all been completed, guns have been positioned and so far there are no available targets.

During our six days travel we had not seen any British tanks or heavy artillery. Plenty of French tanks all as tall as a two storey building but they were not going in the same direction as us, they were on the retreat. They knew they could not stop the German advance; they were running away, perhaps in order to live and fight another day. We did not have that option; we were being used as cannon fodder for the German guns.

Back at the farm area some of the lads were brewing up tea. We had the use of the barn. It was like a Butlins holiday camp, nothing to do and all day to do it. We did have look-out in the trenches facing the woods. It is 16:00 hours, still no sign of the enemy, everyone is expecting a night attack.

June 13th 1940 here in Faverolles-la-Campagne it had been an extremely hot day. We had to carry a lot of our equipment plus rifle and ammunition for your own use, plus magazines for the Bren gun; no great hardship more of a nuisance.

The CO would not allow anyone to leave the farm area. The same applied to the other three platoons. Some of the lads including myself wanted to know what was on the other side of the woods but he would not allow any patrols to go out and investigate. We are on the defensive and that's the way he wanted it to stay. Any attacking to be done will be done by the German Army. It had been up to the three platoons to find out if they had completed all their preparations for defence. I used the cycle going to 7 and 9 Platoons; they both could be reached by using the lane.

8 Platoon could only be reached by crossing three or four fields; they were in reserve at the moment. I also had to inform the Platoon Commanders that Major Channer wished to see them at 18:00 hours at the farm area. On my return I informed the CO that his orders had been carried out. I then returned the cycle to the barn.

I did a few hours in one of the trenches. It was very quiet and still very warm. I could see what was going on behind me when I turned my head; the platoon officers had started to arrive at the farm. The meeting was short and sharp; it only lasted about ten minutes. It seems that nothing new had developed and the orders were still the same; last man last bullet situation.

June 13th was nearing its close. German aircraft were flying overhead, the search lights were criss-crossing in the sky, ack-ack guns could be heard above the noise of the planes, the sky was aglow as a dozen fires were blazing, but not in our area, perhaps the outskirts of Paris had been the target. The overhead planes, many of them, seemed to be on a direct line for the coastal area. They could be on their way across the English Channel. They were not looking for us that was for sure, not even the German soldiers knew we were here; the people of Britain did not know we were here. When we left Britain the public were still praising the evacuation of Dunkirk. They also knew that France was on the brink of collapse. Someone should have told the British Government they would gain nothing by appeasement towards the French, by doing so they could lose two Divisions of British Infantry.

It was almost midnight when the lights of a vehicle were seen coming up the farm lane. We were ready to deal with the occupants of the said vehicle; grenades had been taken out of pouches, rifles had been raised ready to fire, but it was not the enemy, it was our own Quarter Master

Sergeant and his ration truck. We had existed on dry rations these last few days and now we were soon to have a hot meal.

It did not take long to unload the ration truck, eight large containers, lids firmly screwed tight, four contained a beef stew, the other four contained rice, they were all labelled stating the contents. Then came bags of French bread, lots more ammunition, grenades, smoke bombs for the 2" mortar, more dry rations, corned beef, beans, biscuits, tea, sugar, condensed milk, chocolates and cigarettes, even packets of toilet paper and a bag of wooden crosses.

Sergeant Major Breame called for the orderlies; this was me and two others. We had to make contact with the three platoons. I was going to 7 Platoon half a mile further down the lane.

I knew the exact spot they were in as I had been twice during daylight hours. Now it was dark; one has to be very careful during the hours of dark. There were over thirty men out there and they all had a bullet up the spout. Some would be nervous, some would be trigger happy and would shoot at their own shadows, so one had to use a bit of common sense. 7 Platoon were guarding their front and their left flank, so you stand a better chance of living a bit longer if you approach them from the rear and to their right, get as near as possible then whistle your favourite tune and when they challenge you make sure you know the password.

In fact I reached them unchallenged. I was the first to speak, I had taken this individual by surprise, I asked him where I would find Lieutenant Lowe, he said about a hundred yards further up the lane. Some of his men were asleep in the ditch; the lieutenant was sitting on an ammunition box.

I told him the QM Sergeant had arrived at the farm area and that he had brought food and other supplies and that Sergeant Major Breame required six of his men to come to the farm area to collect the food containers plus other supplies. It took him some time to find the six available men as his platoon was well spread out. He also sent a corporal with them. I did not come by cycle because I was ordered to escort the men back to the farm area. On their own they may have waked past the entrance to the farm. The food and supplies were collected and the men made their own way back to their platoon.

The QM Sergeant had brought something else with him; the latest items of news. It was the two cooks who travelled with the sergeant. They told us all the latest rumours; the Germans had surrounded Paris, the French had declared it an open city so the Germans could come and go whenever they pleased. They also said that Italy had declared war on Britain and that the 51st Highland Division, stationed in the Maginot Line for the last six months had come out and fought on the beaches at St. Valery-en-Caux, the Germans had entered the Maginot Line through the back door. There were no available ships to take the Highlanders off the beaches so they finally had to surrender.

We also found out that the 1st Canadian Division who was to accompany us landed at Cherbourg, motored down the coast road to the Port of Brest and sailed back to England. Some say that only the 157 Brigade are here, the rest of the 52nd Lowland Division never left Britain so it seems to me that the 157 Brigade was the cheese in the mouse trap, we were the official sacrifice, we were sent here on the belief that the French would carry on fighting. That's why we were under the command of their army.

I can still hear the voice of the old men and women in the streets of Cherbourg. They are still shouting at us.

'Go home, go home la boche, la boche are coming, go home, go home.'

The QM Sergeant and his two men have gone back to Battalion HQ. Perhaps they will come back again tomorrow night with another hot meal, although I very much doubt it.

Back here in the farm area those who had their meal had now to go and relieve the lads who now occupy the trenches. I found myself in one of the forward trenches about fifty yards to the left and twenty yards in front of the farmhouse. It was 02:00 hours, I had been gazing at the trees in front of me; it was a very dense wooded area I was looking at. I suddenly felt very tired. I can't remember when I had a full nights sleep. Most of the lads, like me, could not sleep in daylight hours. Sleep was out of the question when alone and in a trench, so you had to fight hard just to stay awake.

During the hours of darkness the noise of war was everywhere. It did not worry us, you got use to the sounds of artillery fire; this was not our war. We are infantry, we have bayonets on the front of our rifles, but the mortar shells screaming over our heads in both directions are getting closer.

It was not a pitch dark night, there was a partial moon and lots of shadows had been created mostly from the trees. There were also shaded areas that the moonlight could not penetrate and the more you looked at these dark spots the more tricks your eyes played on you. The shadows began to move, they were performing some kind of ritual. They seemed to take both human and animal shape and form; they had become grotesque, distorted and alien, not of this world.

With a sudden jerk of the head you realise that you must have closed your eyes for a fraction of a second. You have let your mind wander; your daydreams could have been the start of your nightmares and could have been the death of you. It is the Germans who will try and stick a bayonet in your guts not aliens from outer space.

It had been a long spell of watching and waiting for something to happen and now with the morning light everything was bright and clear again, the shadows had gone. No one had appeared out of the woods during the hours of darkness but the feeling that you were being watched was very strong.

It was the platoon sergeants job to make sure that his men had a spell away from the trenches to get as much sleep as possible and a fair share of rations.

Aside from the noise of war the farm area and its inhabitants were very quite on this beautiful morning 14th June 1940.   However it did not stay that way for long.

It was bout 11:00 hours when we heard someone shout.

'Bloody hell the Germans are coming'.

Chapter 3

All eyes turned towards the woods, everyone took up their positions. The Germans were coming out from between the trees and they seemed to stop at the edge of the wood forming one long line, perhaps fifty or sixty of them. We knew we had to hold our fire until the order was given. They spread themselves out and about two feet separated one from the other. They wore their long ankle length grey coats. They walked slowly away from the cover of the trees, both hands on their rifles, fixed bayonets.

We had expected to hear an almighty roar as they charged towards us, but there was no roar and no charge. Just a slow steady walk, they got closer to each other, the farmhouse was their objective. It was uncanny. What were they trying to do, scare the living daylights out of us? Did they expect us to get up and run for our lives? Did they know we were waiting for them?

My own personal feeling was that these were not the mighty Germans that had swept through Holland, Belgium and now France. They were zombies. Not the kind that had risen from the dead. They were the dull stupid type who could not think for themselves. Maybe they were doped up to their eyeballs. My thoughts were broken when the shout of 'Fire' was heard. So the two Bren guns and about thirty rifles opened fire at those wearing the German uniform. Maybe they were not Germans. They could have been any nationality forced to wear the German uniform and made to walk in front of any attack.

The firing continued for a minute or two, there had been no given order to cease firing, each one just stopped when there were no enemies left standing. How many had died, how many lay wounded how many had dropped to the ground pretending to be dead when the first shots were fired? We never really found out. The order we got was that if any of the Germans started to crawl back towards the trees, let them. If they crawled towards us, shoot them. Like us they carried hand grenades. Theirs could be thrown much further because they had a long wooden handle. We called them potato mashers and they were almost within throwing distance.

7 Platoon had not come under fire neither had 8 Platoon. The CO ordered 8 Platoon to come and join HQ and as they made their way towards us they came under German sniper fire. Two

lads had been hit. The tree tops were searched, with the aid of binoculars, movement was spotted to the right of us. We opened fire with the Bren guns and rammed the top of the trees. The snipers were either hit, or they decided it was safer on the ground, we heard no more sniper fire. For the next four hours it was very quiet at the farm, we could move about a little more freely.

But we could hear the mortar fire, it was to our right. It seemed that 'B' Company, at Portes was being attacked.

Our Sergeant Major had told some of the lads to prepare a meal of some kind and to make tea. Most of us had been given iron rations, tins of corned beef, and hard biscuits. We had eaten all the French bread left over from the night before, but our last cup of tea was at 09:00 hours. A mug of tea can do a lot of good and help to boost morale. A mug of hot sweet tea and a cigarette, you feel you could take on the whole German Army.

We never got that mug of tea. The Germans were coming out of the woods again, this time they came out running, moving much faster. But not fast enough, we did not wait for the order to fire, we opened fire, the moment we seen them; we did not wait to see the white of their eyes.

Some lucky ones made it back to the safety of the woods. As long as we had the Bren guns and the ammunition, no German would cross those four hundred yards. There was absolutely no cover except for the bodies that lay there. No one tried making a third frontal attack. They decided to bomb us instead, using something similar to our two inch mortar. The shells came from behind the woods and over the tops of the trees. The first half-a-dozen fell in front of us, those Germans who had been shot, were not being blown apart. The next two or three shells went right over the farmhouse, 8 Platoon were lucky they had moved from their original position.

There must have been a German on top of one of the trees, directing the fire for the mortar crews as they now had the range and the elevation. We heard the screams as the next shell claimed a number of victims. The second and third shell set the barn on fire, that put paid to our long awaited brew up. The next two shells hit the farmhouse, 8 Platoon stayed in the trenches, some of HQ personnel helped to carry the wounded to the safety of another ditch.

The farmer and his wife were lucky they had left the area before the Germans had attacked. Not so lucky for the Sergeant Major and some of his men who had taken up position in the farmhouse. The two first aid men had a very busy time trying to dress the wounded. Most of the ammunition had been taken out of the barn before the attack but the food and the cycle had gone up with the barn.

The shelling had stopped. Were the Germans waiting for us to fly the white flag or were they giving us time to take our wounded and go. But go where? According to Major Channer this was the end of the line, we were no longer on the Isle of Mull on a ten day stint.

We were now in a 'last man last bullet' situation. The barn and the farmhouse were still ablaze, we made no attempt to put them out.

As I said, the shelling had stopped, but we still had the odd sniper fire. We kept firing a few rounds into the woods, now and again mainly to let the Germans know we were still here. But moral was at a very low ebb. We were all feeling the strain, lack of sleep, lack of proper food. We knew the Germans would attack again and again, so no matter how long we held this group of Germans up they were going to win in the end, so we would either finish up dead, or in a prisoner of war camp. I did not want to finish up like the lads in the ditch, with shrapnel wounds in arms, legs or stomach, if you were dead it did not matter how much shrapnel was inside you.

We were in a very tight situation, yet as far as I know no one thought of deserting or running away. If we had been of French nationality, we could have dropped our weapons and returned to our home town, to our families and friends, knowing the Germans, very soon would occupy the whole of France, so why stay and be killed. However we were not French. And the situation we now found ourselves in was not of our own making. Even the French peasants knew that; they knew we were like lambs going to the slaughter, that's why they told us to go home.

'Go home' they said 'go home, le boche is coming'.

They knew nothing could stop the advancing German Army. The British Government also knew the Germans could not be stopped. We were not sent to France to stop the Germans, but just to hold them up for a couple of days more, it seemed like our lot were expendable.

The first aid chaps had told the CO we had eleven dead, and many injured; some of the minor wounded rejoined the rest of the lads.

I had been with 'C' Company for the last four months. I knew most of the lads in HQ, also the NCO and the officers. I had drunk with some of the lads, played cards with others, yet the fact was that some of them had been badly wounded, and some of them were no longer alive. This had no real effect on me; all I could say was poor bloody sods. Exactly the same words I used when I saw the lads on the beaches of Dunkirk. And when the Germans made their attack on us, and got riddled with bullets, we all knew why we were here. To kill. Or be killed.

It was about 18.30 hours on this 14th day of June that the Germans started shelling us again. There was nothing we could do about it, we did have a two inch mortar, but we did not have a target. A mile long wood in front of us, we did not know the depth, and we did not have an observation post. We were under the shell-fire for about twenty minutes, then the Germans came out of the woods, they had pushed some cattle out in front of them.

Maybe they thought this would give a bit of cover, but we were ordered to resume firing, the cows scattered and the Germans ran back to the woods. I was thinking that the next attack would be under the cover of darkness, and perhaps it would be the last one.

But I was wrong. They say that God acts in mysterious ways, or was it the Battalion Commander who sent the angel to our rescue.

He was not the type that had wings. In fact he was more like one of the Hells Angels. He came on wheels, he drove his motorbike into the farm area, skidded to a halt, and he was shouting.

'Who's in charge?'

Major Channer came forward and said "I am".

The dispatch rider gave a verbal message from BN HQ because the French are seeking armistice with the Germans. The new orders are now every man for himself. It was unbelievable, here we were ready to fight until the end and now we had a choice, stay and fight or get the hell out of it. Major Channer decided on the latter.

First he said the rest of the Company had to be warned. There was myself and only another orderly still standing. I knew the location of 7 Platoon and he did not, so I went. The only means of transport, the cycle, was in the barn when the shell set it on fire. 7 Platoon was, as I have said before, half a mile further down the farm lane. It was a lovely evening for a walk but I ran most of that half mile. It was 19:30 hours, still light, would be for a few more hours. I arrived at 7 Platoons position but I could not warn them because they were no longer there. I could see boxes of ammo, the anti-tank rifle, lying in the ditch, cooking utensils, gas masks, webbing material, lots of litter. No dead or wounded. It looks like 7 Platoon had it cushy. They had not passed me. Further down the lane, would take them to the village of Faverolles-la-Campagne. Or did they go some other way?

I can honestly tell you I felt more scared at that moment than I did when the Germans were attacking us. Maybe it was the feeling of being alone, and I was alone, and out of breath. The half mile had taken it out of me. Then leaning my back against the hedge I lit a cigarette. I did not have to think what I was going to do next, I already knew; get away from the woods and the farm area. Faverolles-la-Campagne was not in the direction I was going so that was out of the question. The farm lane would soon be occupied by German vehicles. That only left me with one option, cross country in a north westerly direction.

I did not finish that cigarette, I flicked what was left of it high into the air, I did not see it fall, I was on my way across the field on my left. Still a lot of gunfire going on, I had been walking and running for about twenty minutes. I was halfway across a cornfield when I heard the machine gun, bullets were whistling over my head. The corn was about four foot high. I ran the rest of the way all doubled up. I was heading for the cover of another wooded area. I had almost reached it when I stumbled over what I knew was a body. I heard the grunt so I knew it was a live body.

The body belonged to one of 7 Platoon, he was alright, not injured in any way. I sat down beside him and he said he was running across the field trying to catch up with his platoon when the machine gun opened fire. He took cover in the corn and was going to stay there until it got dark. I asked him who had told 7 Platoon to move. He said a dispatch rider had told the Lieutenant and that he was on his way to warn the rest of the Company. So 7 Platoon had been warned before HQ. That's why I found the place deserted.

The Lieutenant knew that the Germans had attacked the farm area and that the farm was set alight. He had the same idea as me, which was to take to the fields, keep one step ahead of the Germans. So I had caught up with one member of 7 Platoon; would I catch up with the rest? The machine gun fire had stopped, I told the other lad I was going towards the woods. He came with me. When we reached the safety of the woods I decided to get rid of some unwanted items. I told the other chap to do the same. By the way his name was Peter.

We threw away our gas masks, our small packs and our gas capes. We kept our steel helmets, webbing with bayonet and two pouches, bandolier of .303 ammunition and two hand grenades, one in each pouch. I also had a tin of corned beef, a packet of hard tack and some cigarettes, that's why I kept the pouches. Peter was quite willing to let me take the initiative and we were ready to leave when we heard the noise, and someone was approaching. We hid behind the trees.

The sun had gone down but it was still light, we could hear the sound of snapping twigs then the sound of voices. It was not long before the owners of the voices came into view. They wore British uniforms, they were three in number. They had not seen us, neither did they hear us. We could have let them walk past; instead we stepped from behind the trees and ordered them to reveal their identities. The smallest of the three had three chevrons on both arms of his tunic; the other two were private soldiers. We still kept our rifles pointing at them, we had heard stories of German troops wearing British uniform in order to penetrate behind our lines and create havoc, so we were taking no chance.

The Sergeant belonged to the same Battalion as us, he was a member of the Intelligence Section. His name is Anderson, a native of Glasgow. He knew the movements of the brigade. Before the war he was employed with the Glasgow Tram-Way Corporation. So after a little more questioning, Peter and I agreed he was who he said he was. The other two lads had been in a French hospital with stomach trouble. They got out before any German attacks. They had been wandering around for some time, they had met the Sergeant six hours ago, and they both belonged to the Pioneer Corps. I asked the Sergeant what he had been doing prior to our meeting the other two lads. He said his Commanding Officer had sent him out on patrol in order to locate the German positions.

I had no time for sergeants; I did not trust them, and they would lie through their teeth in order to protect their chevrons.

So I said to Peter 'Let's go before it gets too dark, let's get out of these woods'.

It was then that Sgt. Anderson pulled out his revolver, he said 'You are both coming with us, the more of us together, the better chance we have of staying alive'.

It was very lucky for Sergeant Anderson that he did not point the revolver at us, he only waved it in the air, as my rifle was pointing at his private parts. He was just trying to demonstrate that he was the superior one amongst us regarding rank.

Remember I told you about Harry,* the small businessman, he set his own factory on fire, and all the time he was doing it, he was shaking in his boots, he was dead scared. Well Sergeant. Anderson was not a small businessman; he was just a small sergeant. He too was dead scared.

I said 'I don't know where you are going, but Peter and I are going to try and catch up with our Company'.

Anderson said 'We are going up the front line to make contact and join the first regiment we see'.

I said 'If you keep going in the direction you are headed the regiment you meet will be wearing German uniforms, we have just left a number of our lads lying dead in a ditch less than two mile away'.

Peter and I were running away from the Germans, we knew where the Germans were, the wee Sergeant and his two men were also running away from the Germans only they did not know where the Germans were, so they were like the

*From Ye Olde Antique Shoppe

three blind mice, running around in circles. If they kept going in the same direction they were going in, they would lose more than just their tails.

I said, and I don't know why I had not said it before, 'You three have not heard the latest news'.

They did not know what I was talking about. The wee Sergeant said 'What news?'

So I told them that France is seeking armistice with the Germans and that the British war office had announced a message to all British troops in France and the message is 'Every man for himself'.

I knew the way we had come to Faverolles-la-Campagne as I have seen all of the French maps that led us there, and I knew the way back. If the Company is without transport, we would catch up with them.

'Peter and I are going the same way as the rest of the Company so if any of you wish to come along you are welcomed to do so' I said. I had convinced them that I knew what I was doing, now I had to prove it, and find that road.

We set off at a good steady pace, we were now out of the wood. I could see the land in front of us. Mostly open fields, it was slow going finding gaps in the hedgerows, I did not want to cross too many open fields, just in case we were spotted. When I seen a farmhouse, similar to the one now occupied by the Germans, it seemed to be vacated and devoid of any stray Germans. To be on the safe side, I kept about two hundred yards to the left of the farmhouse. When we drew level with the farm, I knew that the lane we were standing on would lead us to the main road. So I decided to use the lane to reach the road I was looking for, besides it was getting too dark for crossing any more fields. Within a very short space of time we had reached the end of the lane. We are now standing in the middle of the road.

The road was deserted, not many miles to our left were the farmhouse, the German troops and the dead and wounded of both armies. Had the Germans stopped at the farmhouse in order to bury the dead and tend to the wounded?

Sergeant Anderson tried once to more to assert his authority by suggesting that we should have two lads walking in front, him in the middle and the other two at the rear walking backwards. This was dismissed as ludicrous, we did not have the time for *silly* walks. We had to put as many miles as possible between us and the Germans and our main aim was to catch up with the retreating British Army.

There was still a lot of shellfire to be heard. Tracer bullets could be seen streaking across the sky and lots of fires could be seen, mostly away in the distance. There was still a little bit of daylight, it would not last much longer. We covered about eight mile, at a steady pace, sometimes jogging but mostly walking. Visibility was not too bad, the light of the moon created shadows as we passed wooded areas. I could see it was time to call a halt, the pace did not suit everyone, and some kept lagging behind. I opened a tin of corned beef and a packet of hard tack and shared them with the others as they had no food. I also passed round the cigarettes. The wee sergeant was a non smoker which led me to believe there must be other things besides smoking that led to stunted growth.

During our eight mile trek we passed a number of farmhouses. As they were well away from the road and showed no signs of life we did not waste time investigating. We were trying to avoid trouble, not cause it. We also passed the road that has taken us to Les Buisson. At the moment I am sitting on a three foot high wall, the other lads are sitting on the ground with their backs against the wall. When I look round I can see the river below; we had bathed in the river and eaten apples from the orchard on the banks of the river.

We had stopped for well over half an hour; it was time to move on again. We still had the road to ourselves, had passed no one and no one had passed us. The German infantry must have been lacking in transport as no vehicle came anywhere near us. The shelling had more or less ceased for the time being, but more fires seemed to be blazing in the distance. It was now 03:00 hours on 15th June 1940.

We had only gone another four or five miles, Peter and I had to slow down very often as the other three kept lagging behind. I did not have any of the maps as they were in the bicycle carrier when the barn was set on fire. We had passed a number of villages coming here that we must pass through again very soon.

Eventually we did arrive at the first of these villages. The whole place was in darkness and as we walked in single file through the village I had the feeling that hundreds of pairs of eyes were watching. We were only yards away from some of the houses; it seemed as if the whole village had been deserted. Not even the barking of a stray dog interrupted the sound our army boots were making. No transport could be seen, not even the odd bicycle. We left the village as we found it.

Back on the road again we stopped many times for short break; most of them unnecessary. If Peter and I had been on our own we would have covered a much greater distance. I was beginning to have doubts about catching up with the Company. We passed another village just off the main road. It did not interest us so we kept on going. The morning light had come upon us but I can't remember hearing the dawn chorus. I think even the birds had deserted the countryside.

After more miles of travel we turned a bend in the road and in the distance we could see yet another village. We retraced our steps and had a bit of a confab because in front of the village was a barricade.

The wee sergeant wanted to use the ditch at the side of the road as cover and move slowly towards the barricade. I did not agree. We had seen the sentry at the barricade and if he was doing his job properly he would have seen us. The barricade was facing the enemy lines and in my opinion they were looking out for Germans. If we had been Germans without transport we may have used the ditch as cover, but we were not Germans. Peter and I slung our rifles over our shoulders and walked down the road in single file ready to jump into the ditch if fired on.

The sentry was standing with his rifle at the on guard position. As we drew nearer he lowered it, we quickened our step and reached the barricade. It was handshakes all round.

The sentry pointed towards the village and said 'English Officer' and bowed in salutation.

He knew V.I.P's. when he saw them! With a graceful sweep of his arm he waved us through.

Someone said 'I could have kissed that French soldier when I first seen him'.

'Why didn't you?' someone else said.

We walked towards the centre of the village and there stood a monument in honour of those who fell in the last war. It had a drinking well but no drinking vessel. That did not stop us from having our fill. A group of French soldiers approached us; once more it was handshakes all round. Among them was English speaking French officer; it did not matter who he was as he could speak our lingo. He told us that as far as he knew the British troops were going to take up a defence position about ten miles from where we were. He also told me where he had last seen them. The other four lads were trying to scrounge some food whilst I was talking to the officer. He had only one truck and this was to take himself and his men to safety. He told us he was sorry he could not provide us with transport.

He pointed to a large building which looked like an aircraft hanger. He told me that at the first sign of the Germans he was going to blow it up rather than have it fall into German hands. He also said we had time to help ourselves to some of its contents. It was mostly a food warehouse; tins, canvas sacks and boxes as well as lots of beer and liqueur. I took two packets of biscuits, some dark chocolate and two bottles of beer and the other lads took what they wanted. The wee sergeant had a large bottle of whisky which he started to drink and he put some beer bottles in his tunic pockets.

We spent over half an hour at the village eating and drinking as well as having a bit of a wash at the well.

We thanked the French for their hospitality, shook hands with all those present and left. As we passed through the rest of the village not a soul was to be seen. Perhaps they would find a safer haven in the large cities and towns.

Back on the road now we did not have to act with caution with the French behind us and the British somewhere in front. We did not have to worry what might be round the next bend but speed was essential if we wanted to catch up. The slowest man was holding the others up and it was not always the same man. There seemed to be a `could not care less` attitude and I had seen Peter trying to urge them on. The wee sergeant stopped many times to sip at his whisky. We tried to get him to throw it away but he would not part with his bottle.

I had gained a lot of information from the French officer. As well as learning where the British were last seen he also told me that some British troops had passed through the village on board a small lorry; but they had not stopped. Shortly after that a platoon of British troops were allowed through the barricade, stopped at the village and were given rations. After a short space of time the lorry came back and picked up the rest of the platoon. That had been three hours ago. We would never catch up with them if they kept going in this leap frog manner. I kept most of this information to myself as no one else seemed to be concerned.

It was approximately 08:00 hrs when we left the last village. We have covered about five miles since then. This has taken well over two hours. Peter and I have been over a hundred yards in front of the other three just to try and make them catch up. Its no use, we have to stop and wait for them. I think the wee sergeant is encouraging the other two lads to stay near him; the drink is now taking its toll on him. The sun is very warm and makes walking difficult, the lack of proper sleep doesn't help. We can't help them in any way. The sergeant was only carrying a belt and a revolver, no other equipment.

The two lads from the Pioneer Corps had no equipment and no rifle. Peter and I had grenades, ammunition, webbing equipment, rifles and bayonets. The fact that we were infantry and twenty five miles was the average distance we marched each week during training stood us in good stead for the kind of thing like running away from the Germans.

It was at 11:00 hrs as we turned a bend in the road that we heard the sound of traffic. We could see the crossroad ahead and the moving vehicles. When we reached the crossroads Peter and I stopped; I took out my cigarettes, gave Peter one and we lit up. The road we were on was much wider than the one we had just come off. The vehicles were mostly vans and lorries and a few cars and farm carts piled high with furniture.

They were all going in the same direction and that was toward the French Belgium border.

There were also the odd French soldiers who wanted to keep walking, hands deep in pockets, heads and eyes fixed on the ground. The outlook for them was bleak, perhaps slave labour in some ammunition factory or maybe forced to wear the German uniform.

The other three had joined Peter and me. They were amazed at the amount of traffic and wanted to know if they could get a lift, saying that the road must lead to some big town. I said if I get a lift I will take it, but it has to be in the direction I am going in and that direction is straight across. However, the wee sergeant thought it would be better to go with the flow of traffic. I said each man can make his own choice. I finished my cigarette and asked Peter if he was coming. He said he was so we crossed over and continued our walk.

We had only gone a couple of hundred yards when Peter looked round and said 'they are coming behind us'.

I guessed they would be. We passed a number of French farm people still working on the land. We did not converse with any of them as I did not want false information regarding directions. I was quite happy to stay on this road. We had covered another four miles when we heard the sound of vehicles coming from behind us, travelling in the same direction as ourselves. We stopped as they came near and tried to hitch a lift but they would not stop. They sped by at about sixty miles an hour, a convoy of eight jeep-like vehicles each pulling a 25 pounder gun and a battery of British artillery. Some of the co-drivers waved at us as they passed by; the fact that they did not stop did not worry me a great deal. I guessed it was they who had been shelling the night before and would be doing it again in order to slow the Germans down. The wee Glasgow sergeant did not see it that way; he shook his fist at them as they passed by. To console himself he took another swig out of the bottle of whisky he still carried in his hand. Anyone could see he was a little tipsy. However, he could still walk, but at his own pace. We had only gone a couple more miles when we approached the outskirts of a fairly large village. It could have been a small town; who cares it was civilization at last. The war had not touched this part as there was no destruction of any kind.

It was 13:00 hrs on the 15th June when we arrived here at St Anne's village. The people were going about their business as usual. They knew the Germans were coming to take over their country; they could do nothing about it; they carried on as normal. The shops were open and as I, Peter and the sergeant still had some French money we bought bread and cheese and some wine. Nobody went without as we shared everything.

Some of the people greeted us in their normal fashion, with words and waving of the hands. We must have looked a sorry sight to them as we had not shaved for days, our uniforms had creases in all the wrong places; we were in a mess.

We sat on the pavement and devoured some of what we had purchased. We ate like pigs, filling our bellies just in case our next meal was somewhere in the distant future. After we had eaten we strolled up the main road and went into one or two shops. They had almost run out of stock, the French people must have filled up their cupboards. I bought some apples and in the bakers I bought a few cakes that would not go stale too quickly. I stuffed them in my pouch beside the hand grenades.

We had just left the bakers shop and were ready to start walking once more when suddenly an army lorry stopped outside the shop. A lieutenant and sergeant jumped out of the cabin. The lieutenant pushed past us and went into the bakers. He gave us a very dirty look; no wonder as most of what we had bought was stuffed down our tunics. I did not look too bad as I only had apples. The wee Glasgow sergeant looked like he was ready to give birth at any moment. He still had some whisky left in the bottle that he was hiding behind his back. The sergeant who was with the officer told us to get back to our units as the town was out of bounds to British personnel. The wee Glasgow sergeant had turned away; he knew he was unfit to talk to anyone. I told him where we had come from and how far we had travelled. He told us St Anne's was out of bounds and that we must keep moving. He did say that the infantry was about two miles down the road.

So once more we decided to move on. We were almost in contact with our units. How had we managed to get this near to "C" Company? They must have stopped during the hours of darkness whereas we had never stopped walking, apart from stopping here and there for a bit of a rest. We had never slept; may have closed our eyes for a few moments but that was all. We had been walking from 20:00 hrs on the 14th June and it was now 14:00hrs on the 15th June, a total of eighteen hours. Previous to that we had very little sleep at the farmhouse. As we walked the last few miles that would lead us to our units I did feel sleepy but at moment sleep was the last thing on my mind. As I turned round and looked at the wee sergeant his eyes seemed to be closed. The whisky mixed with the French beer and wine had taken effect. He was now more or less sleep walking.

We had only been walking for about one hour when we came across the first lot of infantry. They belonged to our brigade but were not part of our battalion. They were the 6th Battalion H.L.I. I spoke to one of the officers. He did not give us a very warm welcome; in fact he treated us as if we had leprosy.

I expect he had enough on his plate looking after his own people. Perhaps he did not want to add the boozy five to his collection. I was not going to stay where I was not wanted and he did tell me that the 5th battalion was four miles further down the road so I thanked him, saluted him and turned away.

I said to the other four 'let's go'.

Only Peter got to his feet. The wee sergeant and the two men stayed sitting on the grass near the wood that concealed the 6th Battalion. The sergeant said they wanted a rest before going any further so we bid them a soldier's farewell and told them not to get lost again. The wee Glasgow sergeant would have to sober up a lot before speaking to any officer.

We soon found the 5th Battalion, "C" Company was a mile further down the road. They also had taken refuge in a large wooded area near the side of the road. It took time to recognise some of the lads; they looked terrible, more like old men than lads of twenty. They were sprawled out all over the place with rifles lying on the ground. It looked as if they had given up, just waiting for the Germans to come and round them up and take them to the nearest prisoner of war camp. Admitted, some looked worse than others. The wounded with their blood stained bandages; two had head wounds, others had arm or leg wounds. Split trousers revealed the field dressings; some red with blood.

I found the CO Major Channer. He seemed to have aged; his hair was almost grey. I don't know if it was the lack of hair cream or the fact that he had lost three quarters of his company and he had no idea what was going to happen to the fourth quarter. Perhaps the responsibility was too much for one man to carry. He was sitting with his back leant against a tree when we approached him. He was amazed to see us. He stood up and shook hands with us both, very pleased that we had managed to rejoin the company.

He said 'we had come a long way, over 60 kilometres from Faverolles-la- Campagne to St Anne's'.

He said sit down to both of us. He wanted to know what happened at 7 Platoon, he remembered that I went there. So I told him that when I got there 7 Platoon had gone.

I looked at Peter and said 'Peter told me that the dispatch rider had warned them first and was then going to warn HQ. It did not make sense for me to go back to the farmhouse as I knew the Germans had now occupied it. I thought 7 Platoon had turned right and made their escape via Faverolles-la-Campagne. I decided to go cross country in order to reach the main road and while crossing the fields I met Peter'. The CO interrupted me by saying to Peter, 'you are a very lucky young man, you are the only member of 7 Platoon to be here'. He added 'the others may turn up later'.

I told CO Major Channer all about the wee Sergeant and his two men. I had assured them I knew the way to go to reach the road. They were heading towards the farmhouse and going to join the first regiment they met. If they had not met me they would have had a big surprise when they reached the farm. I told him about meeting the English speaking French Officer. CO Major

Channer then told me about his troops passing through the village in a small lorry. He also said he only got three or four miles out of it after leaving the village. He said we pushed it into a ditch, the engine had busted. I told him about the catering officer and the sergeant we met outside the bakers shop in St Anne's. We were then told to get back to our units, that's what we had been trying to do for the last eighteen hours, make contact. He said infantry units were four miles further on.

When I had told CO Major Channer what he wanted to know I thought "now it's my turn to ask a few questions".

I asked him 'what happened at the farmhouse'.

He said 'the shelling had stopped',

He had ordered everyone into the farm lane. The Germans had come out of the woods and were crossing the fields.

CO Major Channer said 'we ran and we found the dispatch rider. He must have been hit by a mortar. He was dead. We reached the end of the lane and on to the road. The Germans did not give chase'.

I asked him about the quarter master sergeant and the ration truck. He told me he has not been seen since the night he brought the hot meal.

I said 'what about 9 Platoon, are they all here?'

CO Major Channer said 'we could not locate them'.

Now, I just had to ask him the sixty four dollar question. 'Why are we waiting Sir?'

His answer to that was that the Royal Army Service Corps has been notified of our position. We are waiting for transport to arrive.

I said 'that sounds good'. I also thought to myself they had better hurry up or the Germans will be doing the picking up.

Only thirty four of the lads had made it from the farmhouse. That included Peter and me, so out of a company of approximately one hundred and twenty one individuals, only thirty four are left. We know some are dead and some are wounded. Perhaps 7 and 9 Platoons have found a safe haven with other British units. They could have been taken prisoners, it remains to be seen.

It was around 17:00 hrs when we had finished talking to the major.

His final words were 'go find a nice tree and lean your backs against it; you will be here for some time yet.'

Yes, we spent another night in the woods under a starry sky. There had been no need to post sentries; this task had been allocated to another battalion. At the moment we are in reserve. I had a good nine hours sleep, so it is now 06:00 hrs 16th June 1940 on the outskirts of a place called St. Anne's about sixty miles from the farmhouse and in the opposite direction, one hundred and eighty miles from the port of Cherbourg.

This was, or will be, our ninth day in France. It no longer belongs to the French; they have handed over complete power to the German N.A.Z.I. Party. The skies above are controlled by them and the bombers flying overhead belong to them. It's only the contents that they are giving away, perhaps to the Londoners.

We had no breakfast this morning but we had something better. We had received word that our transport was on its way and would be here before midday. The news cheered everyone up a bit, except for a few doubting Thomas'. I think at this time I was one of those. The coastline was a long way off, the road maybe choked with refugees and broken down vehicles. German planes above and the German army perhaps less than forty mile away could be here within the hour. I could not understand why they were not already here as we had left them a wide open road.

I had shared the apples and cakes with a few other lads from HQ the evening before, no one had eaten today. No one complained, no shouts of 'When do we eat' could be heard. Shortly after 10:00 hrs a shout was heard.

'The transport is here'.

It was a convoy of R.A.S.C. Troop Carriers, maybe twenty or more. Some completely covered over with their waterproof canvas rigging, others were without cover. As they went straight passed our lot there were shouts of surprise.

'Where are they going?'

We knew there were other units, perhaps they were picking them up first. The road was very narrow and the drivers of the trucks had gone ahead in order to find a turning point. It was not long before the first lorry stopped when he saw us standing at the side of the road. It was an open truck with seating accommodation for twenty two, eleven on each side, two standing with their backs to the cab, eight more sat on the floor, it was a tight squeeze, even tighter when they put the tailboard up. The major and the lieutenant from 8 Platoon sat in the cab beside the driver. So what was left of `C` Company were all aboard one truck. We were no longer under the command of the French Army. It was not the British who requested an armistice so our obligation to the French was well and truly over. 157 Brigade was now part of the Norman Force and our orders were all persons will evacuate to the UK as soon as possible.

We moved off as soon as we were loaded on the truck. One of the other drivers took over the lead. We have now got the number 2 spot in the convoy. This was very handy as we stopped many times during our journey, mainly in very populated areas. At our request to the French civilians for food, we were given bread and cheese, fruit and even flowers.

One of our early stops was at a place called Domfront where all the trucks took on petrol. It had been a two hour hold up and when we finally moved off at 14:00 hrs we were one man less. It happened like this: because the journey had been very rough on the way here with the sudden starting and stopping some of the chaps had used their rifles to sort of counter balance to offset the jolting. This particular chap who was seated had the butt of his rifle on the floor of the truck, his two hands across the muzzle of the rifle, his head was bent forward and his chin was resting on his hands. Some of the chaps who were squatting on the floor of the truck decided to stand up. They wanted to see what was going on and we believe in doing so, perhaps one chance in a million, the trigger of his rifle had been nudged by hand, by foot or the movement of another rifle, we just don't know. The safety catch of the rifle had not been engaged; there was a bullet in the breach.

There is no need for me to give you the gory details. There was no immediate enemy in the vicinity. All bullets should have been in the magazine and the safety catch should have been engaged. His was not.

As I said our truck was stationery at the time. Major Channer came out of the cab as a crowd of French gathered round at the sound of the rifle fire. When the CO had been told what happened he immediately told all of us to put the safety catches on. One or two did so, the rest all had the catches engaged. Then he said to reject the bullets from the breach. Not one bullet fell to the floor of the truck. The CO had made sure that what had happened would not occur a second time.

Amongst the crowd that had gathered round the truck were two French nuns. When they were told that the lad was dead they said they would make sure that he had a decent burial. Not knowing when we would be moving, the body was lifted off the truck and placed on the pavement; someone provided a white sheet. The CO gave the nuns a pile of French money. They did not want to take it but he insisted. One of them had gone away and ten minutes later she returned accompanied by two men pushing a handcart. We watched it being pushed down the road and out of sight. `C` Company was now reduced to thirty three men. The CO had one more identity disc to add to his collection.

During our 180 mile dash to the coast we passed through a number of French towns; St Hilaire, Avranches, Coutances then on to Cherbourg. We broke the speed limit many times and at other times we could have walked faster than the trucks were moving.

Chapter 4

We arrived at Cherbourg on the night of 17th June and could not get near to the dock area. The convoy was halted by the Military Police. We learned that the harbour area was packed solid with abandoned and broken down vehicles. There was only one ship and it was already full. After a lot of discussion with the Military Police the CO told us to march to the harbour. Only the first four trucks were allowed to off load, the rest were diverted down the coast road to the port of Brest.

We marched to the docks and were ushered through the barriers past a long queue of civilians who were hoping to get on board. The vessel was a cargo ship no bigger than a cross channel ferry. The deck was packed tight with troops. This seemed to be the only vessel afloat; there were others damaged and half submerged.

The CO said 'Right lads find a space for yourselves.'

The troops already aboard were hugging the rails of the ship. German planes were in the vicinity but not directly above and ack ack guns could be heard; the planes could dive at any moment.

The Military Police came on the ship and pushed everyone into a tighter mass. I managed to find a space near the deckhouse; others pushed passed me. There were two large wooden pallets on deck, contents about six foot high, completely covered in tarpaulin. Someone cut the ropes that secured the tarpaulin and pulled it away to reveal a large number of cardboard containers which, when opened, revealed tens of thousands of English cigarettes. Could it have been a black market deal? They were certainly under cover; the cigarettes were now coming in all directions. I stopped passing them when a chap beside me told me nobody wanted any more. I had two hundred John Players so I threw away the French rubbish.

Other Military Police who were on the dockside came aboard and the gangway was removed. The ship pulled away from the harbour and then, I believe, the anchor was dropped. Nobody knew what was happening; we were just bobbing about in the water but going nowhere. We were a sitting target for any German fighter plane on a moonlight patrol.

We heard rumours that the Captain refused to take the ship out to sea as he said the Germans knew he was here and would sink him as soon as he was clear of the harbour.

We left Cherbourg at 02:00 hrs on the 18th June aboard the Manxman. I am led to believe that she was the last ship to leave Cherbourg bound for England during those early years. I think those who came back were very, very lucky because the people or person who ordered us out did not expect us to return. As far as they were concerned we were expendable.

We reached Southampton waters at 06:00 hrs and there was a small committee on the quayside to welcome us. As we stepped down the gangway each man was handed ten cigarettes, a mug of tea and a bread roll; it made a change from the French bread. As my feet touched terra firma I did not kneel down and kiss the ground. However, I did say a silent prayer, not just for myself, but also for the poor sods that did not make it back. As I looked around what did I see? I did not see a cheering crowd, no hero's welcome, no flags flying, again no wives or sweethearts to kiss and greet us. How could we expect them to welcome us back; they did not even know we had gone. Only those at No.10 knew our whereabouts. Besides thanking God for our safe return we also have to thank General Dill, a member of the war cabinet, as it was he who finally convinced the Prime Minister that sending two divisions of infantry to France was a sheer waste of manpower and equipment. France was on the verge of collapse and the two divisions would be needed more in Britain if Hitler invaded. I believe the Canadian Division was recalled and also part of the 52nd Lowland Division before they took part in any action.

On the 17th June 1940 at St Nazarene the liner Lancastria was sunk with 3000 troops aboard.

On the day we left Cherbourg the Germans entered it and on the 19th June Rommel, The German General, paraded through the streets of the town.

The war in France was over for the time being; still, those of us that came back were still alive and ready to fight another day. The monstrous beast of war, his appetite is satisfied for the time being, but it won't be long before he rears his ugly head again, so be on your guard and don't be his next course.

I am now taking you back to Southampton. I told you that `C` Company was down to thirty three in number; I forgot about the two lads that went astray. We were all in the truck at the time when the Military Police halted the convoy. The two lads at the back of our truck, enticed by two French fillies, I don't mean the four legged type, on the promise of a good time, disappeared from our ranks. I hope they found it was worth while.

Many of the lads believed that the invasion of Britain would take place in a matter of weeks so some of them went AWOL –absent without leave. I might have done the same if I had been married and had a family, but I was not married so the thought of absconding never entered my head. Four of the lads went AWOL and that left `C` Company with twenty seven. Five of the lads that had been wounded were taken by ambulance to some hospital, so that left twenty two. The CO and the Lieutenant both disappeared to some officer's quarters; that left twenty of us. I and six others were taken to a school hall and given temporary accommodation. The remaining thirteen went elsewhere. Two weeks later we joined the battalion at Biggleswade.

`C` Company had been reformed. The men came from a reinforcement Company and to me they were all strangers. I no longer wanted to be a member of `C` Company HQ so I joined 9 Platoon. I soon got to know them all. The battalion moved many time. The companies were always stationed miles away from each other. Being out of Co. HQ I no longer had access to battalion orders etc. There was a particular order that I knew nothing about. I missed it completely. It relates to the first page of this book. If I had seen that particular order when it was first issued I could have done something about it, because what took place could have been substantiated at the time. By the time I found out to much water had flowed under the bridge. Too many years have gone by for a wrong to be put right; perhaps the evidence is no longer there.

A little more about myself and `C` Company. One of our moves took us back to Perth Barracks. This was the home of the Black Watch. They were not residing there at the moment; they were taken prisoner by the Germans in northern France so the HLI had temporary use of the premises. It did not last long; we had to get out as a new Black Watch was being established. So `C` Company found themselves in a small village called St Fillans and spent eighteen months in that billet, isolated from the rest of the battalion.

In July of 1942 the battalion, along with many others, boarded the Queen Mary at Southampton and sailed to the Middle East. We ended up in a transit camp in a place called Ismailia. We stayed a month in Moascar transit camp, it was worse than any prison, then me and a few others were sent to the Citadel in Cairo to join the 2nd Battalion HLI. I got to know Cairo well. I also spent two and a half months doing ceremonial guard duties but I was bored stiff. I saw a notice on the board asking for volunteers to join the Eighth Army and I found myself with the 5th Battalion Black Watch, through the North Africa campaign, to Malta, the invasion of Sicily then back to England to train for the invasion of France.

Whilst training in Limehouse, London I received an injury to my hand through no fault of my own. I had to spend six weeks in Poplar Hospital and many months in convalescence. `D` Day took place without me much to my regret, I was sorely disappointed. Later I was attached to the 53rd Italian Labour Battalion which involved mostly the escorting of Italian personnel from London to other parts of the country.

I have not mentioned it before but my rank at the moment is Corporal. I got my first chevron in North Africa and my second in Sicily. The reason I mention that is because a notice appeared on the board in our office. They wanted a full Corporal at the Palace Barracks in Holywood, Co. Down, Northern Ireland. They wanted someone to take responsibility of the confinement of four thousand German prisoners of war during the hours of daylight. I applied and got the post. I had the help of two other lads, John Thompson and George McDonald; they were very good lads.

It was coming near the time for my demobilization; I had been in the barracks for nine months now. I was offered the third chevron if I stay on. How could I take it? I hate sergeants, yes, especially wee ones. So I declined that third chevron. My army days were over, I was a civilian once again.

Chapter 5

I married a girl from Hollywood, had a family, watched them grow up and had three grand children and two great grandchildren (so far). I became a senior citizen in the 90`s and to pass the long winter days I started to write a little of my six war years.

One could find plenty of material regarding the desert warfare, the Invasion of Sicily, but very little, if anything has been written about those who were sent to France on the 7th June 1940. Days after, hundreds of thousands of British, France and Belgium troops were taken off the beaches of Dunkirk. It was and still is all so hush. That was why I contacted Dr Diane Henderson for more information. I wanted to know why we were sent there, who were killed and who were taken prisoner. I also sent her a copy of what took place at the farmhouse in Faverolles-la-Campagne. Dr Henderson told me to read Mountain and Flood. I obtained a copy and there was only a small paragraph relating to the event. This is what it said.

A characteristic experience was that of Sgt. W. Anderson of the Intelligence Section of the 5th carrying a message to `A` Company, then *heavily engaged, he had his motor-cycle put out of action beneath him. Even so he delivered the signal on foot but was unable to take part in the withdrawal as his message had ordered. For some days he lurked behind enemy lines avoiding capture and when he re-joined the unit at St.Annes, far to the westwards, it was with five men he had collected on the way – a solid bit of good soldiering for which he was awarded the Distinguished Conduct Medal.*

There is one more paragraph that relates only to Sergeant Anderson, no other men involved.

Anderson 3313030 Sgt. William 5th Battalion the Highland Light Infantry – France/Belgium 1940. On the 14th June `40 at Fessiere la Cloche the NCO carried the message by motor cycle from Battalion HQ to Company HQ ordering the withdrawal of the Company. He had to approach through a hail of LMG fire which might well have caused him to give up the attempt. His very outstanding courage and coolness undoubtedly saved the lives of every person at Company HQ and by getting the message through he saved the whole Company, which was rapidly being surrounded by overwhelming numbers, from being cut off.

It is impossible to praise too highly his courage.

London Gazette 20.12.1940

You have now read what I have written and the paragraph of the event. Who is telling the truth and who is not?

The commendation printed in the London Gazette regarding Sergeant Anderson and his outstanding courage and coolness while undoubtedly saving lives, and which took place on the 14th June 1940, did not mention the five men he was supposed to have picked up. I wonder why not?

Regarding the paragraph from Mountain and Flood; this book was published in 1950, ten years after the fall of France. So when did Sergeant Anderson start lying and why? Anyone reading the articles would consider Sergeant Anderson to be a very brave man. It would be a terrible thing to think otherwise.

Deep down I had the inner satisfaction of knowing that I helped to save the other four from death or from being taken prisoners. I now feel that I have been cheated. I also know that no matter how many lies the wee Sergeant has told, the truth will still be the truth. It may have been concealed under a pack of lies; perhaps one day it will emerge.

Regarding the commendation given to Sergeant Anderson by the London Gazette; I cannot dispute his entitlement to this as I was not there. `C` Company was ten kilometres from `A` Company and about five kilometres from `B` Company. The Gazette does not state which company the Sergeant gave the message to. It does state that he carried the message from Battalion HQ to Company HQ. He had to approach through a hail of light machine gun fire in order to get the message through.

The report in Mountain and Flood states that his motor cycle was put out of action beneath him, even so, he delivered the signal on foot. He had warned the Company to withdraw but could not take part in the withdrawal himself? He was not wounded, he did not have a broken leg, nor did he lose his boots when the motor cycle was put out of action beneath him. Only he knows the answer.

I know he was not wounded or had a broken leg, or was minus his boots? I also know that he did not lurk behind enemy lines for some days avoiding capture.

On that same day, 14th June 1940 at 19:00 hrs, I spoke to the dispatch rider when he rode into the farm area and asked who was in charge. Major Channer said he was. The messenger said that France was seeking an armistice. I know I have already told you this, but I have repeated it just to emphasize the point. One hour later at 20:00 hrs I challenged Sergeant Anderson to reveal his identity. So when did he lurk behind enemy lines for some days?

How did I know he didn't have a broken leg? I knew because with a lot of encouragement from Peter and me he managed to walk from the outskirts of Faverolles-la-Campagne to St Annes. According to Major Channer this was a distance of fifty nine kilometres; this took the best part of eighteen hours. I am sure if it had just been Peter and I we could have cut that time by five hours. Don't get me wrong, I have no regrets at stopping the Sergeant and his two men as we all arrived safely back in Britain.

When I stopped him in the woods I also robbed him of his superiority. This he did not like one little bit. He did try to regain it once or twice, but to no avail. He had no idea where he was or where he was going. There were no pleasantries between us during our trek; in fact there was practically no conversation between us. He stayed close to the two lads from the Pioneer Corps. using them as a sort of anchor, something to hold on to. I had told them previously and given them assurances, that we would catch up with the Battalion; perhaps I had not fully convinced them.

Things got worse after we left the village that was occupied by the French soldiers. The wee Sergeant, with his whisky and beer, slowed our pace right down. He was putting all our lives in danger. We were still a long way from the nearest troops.

Finally we reached St. Annes and from there, with the information given to us by the other Sergeant, we soon found the first lot of British troops. It was here that we parted company with the wee Glasgow Sergeant and his two men. I bid Sergeant Anderson a soldier's farewell. I had kept my promise that we would catch up with the rest of the troops. It felt good to get him off my back; I had carried him long enough.

I never saw Sergeant Anderson again and I have never spoken to him since. I read a little about him in 1999 when the director for the Scot's at War Trust told me to read Mountain and Flood. What I have written regarding the wee Glasgow Sergeant might never be established. He has built a wall of lies and it is going to be very difficult to break down.

When I stopped Sergeant Anderson in the wooded area we were two miles from the farmhouse which was now occupied by German troops. One of the questions I asked the Sergeant was what he was doing on his own prior to picking up the other two lads six hours previously. His reply was that he had been sent out to try and locate German troop movement. I believe he was telling the truth on this occasion.

But when was he sent out; 12th, 13th or 14th June? We all know where the Germans were on the 14th June so if he was sent out on the 13th, got himself lost, wandered about, picked up the other two lads midday or shortly afterwards on the 14th. I stopped them at 20:00 hrs the same evening, a long, long way away from `A` Company's position.

`C` Company was given the message to withdraw at 19:00 hrs but when did `A` Company get the message and who really delivered it? The commendation states that Sergeant Anderson delivered, it but he himself was unable to take part in the withdrawal, so he lurked behind enemy lines for some days. He was with me the same evening at 20:00 hrs. I left him sitting on the grass verge along with the other two at 15:00 hrs on the 15th June.

He did not know that the French were parleying with the Germans for the purpose of seeking an armistice.

When stopped he said they were going up to join the first unit that he met. I don't think the Germans would have found a uniform to fit him. I did say he was a wee Sergeant.

My son, on my behalf, contacted Dr Diane Henderson, Director of the Scot's at War Trust; this is one of her replies.

Many thanks for your letter and your father's note. There will probably never be a way of resolving what actually happened fifty years ago however, you might like to go to the public record office in Kew, London and look at the Battalion, Brigade and Divisional war diaries which are the official records compiled at the time of what happened. If they exist they will probably not be very detailed but it is certainly worth a try.

You might also like to contact the Regimental Headquarters of the Highland Fusiliers to see if they have any information. I am sure they will be pleased to hold a copy of your father's book in the Regimental records to ensure that his

*account of events is properly recorded. The
address of the RHF RHQ is on the Scot's at
War web site.*

*Best wishes
Yours sincerely
Diane A Henderson*

Dr Henderson ended the letter by thanking
me for all the information given.

The following is the reply I received from the
Regimental Headquarters of the Royal Highland
Fusiliers:

*Many thanks for your letter regarding your
encounter with Sgt. Anderson DCM. I look
forward to reading your account of the incident,
indeed I would be interested in reading your
book, and then I will advise you on the way
forward.
15th September 1999.*

The following is the contents of the second
letter sent by Major Shaw of the Royal Highland
Fusiliers on 13th October 1999.

*5th Bn. HLI 2nd World War   Many thanks for
your letter and a copy of your book relating to*

the incident involving Sgt. Anderson DCM. I would like to see his version of the story before I make up my mind what should be done. However, I would point out that when a DCM is awarded it goes in the chain of command and the person in question is under scrutiny. I cannot understand, if half of what you have written is correct, why you received no recognition from the battalion as people must have reported your handling of the situation.

My reply to the above letter was as follows.

I told my CO Major Channer all about the incident when I caught up with him at St Annes. He had a lot on his plate at the time; he was a very worried man. What I told him went in one ear and out the other.

When we returned to Britain I forgot the whole incident; I never mentioned it to anyone. I never knew Sgt. Anderson had received a medal until I found out in 1999.

The third letter from Major Shaw dated 11th January 2000 is s follows.

5ᵗʰ BN HLI 2ⁿᵈ World War I cannot come to any conclusion regarding the incident involving Sgt. Anderson. I would have liked to have his side of the story. The official version resulted in the award of the DCM. I wonder why you have waited so long to raise this matter as you must have been aware that Sgt. Anderson had been decorated for his bravery in 1940.

Now sixty years later you are disputing the actions leading to the award. Have you anyone who can corroborate your version of events? I await your reply with interest.'

My reply:

Dear Major Shaw
Thank you for your letter of 11ᵗʰ January 2000. I originally wrote to you at the suggestion of Dr Henderson as she thought that you would be able to suggest a way forward so that a conclusion could be reached. Would the official version not be Sgt.Anderson`s version or at least his account incorporated within it?

I was never aware that any awards had been given to the 5ᵗʰ Bn. HLI.

I have to go back to June 1940. We left France on the 18th June aboard the S.S. Manxman. At Southampton thirty one men of `C` Company walked down the gang plank. The rest of the BN had gone to the Port of Brest. Our CO and one other officer had to leave us. The wounded and those suffering from shock were hospitalized and some absconded, but I and four others were billeted in a school house.

When I rejoined `C` Company I no longer wanted to be a member of HQ, so I joined a platoon. I no longer had access to incoming messages, so I knew nothing about the awards. `C` Company had billets in St Fillians near Perth in Scotland. We stayed there for eighteen months along with drill and route marches; we helped the farmers by digging up potatoes etc. Our next move was to Southampton as a Company where we boarded the Queen Mary. The rest of the battalion were also aboard, along with 17,000 other troops.

We reached Port Said and from there to a transit camp in Ismailiya. All officers and non commissioned officers departed and the camp officers took over. From there I was transferred to the 2nd HLI in Cairo. Some months later I asked to join the Eighth Army; I then became a member of the Black Watch.

To cut a long story short; the war ended and I became a civilian and in 1992 I started to write a book and the incident about Sgt. Anderson was part of it. The book covered my six years in the army. Years later I decided to write again, but only about the ten days in France 1940. I wanted to know more about what took place then, so I wrote to Dr Henderson. It was when I read the book Mountain and Flood that I learned about Sgt. Anderson. That was in 1998; the first I had heard of any medal. The London Gazette I read much later which of course does not relate to the five men Sgt. Anderson says he picked up.

Could you possibly suggest what I could do next or if there is any other address I could write to? Also, can I obtain a copy of the official version as I have never read this; I would very much like to do so.

Yours sincerely
Mr J.J. Savage

The fourth letter from Major Shaw as follows:

Regimental Headquarters
The Royal Highland Fusiliers
25th January 2000

<u>Sgt. Anderson DCM 5th HLI</u> There was a disastrous fire here in 1985 which destroyed the bulk of the library and archives and suffice to say no original records appertaining to the award of the DCM to Sgt. Anderson remains here. I cannot say who put Sgt. Anderson forward for a decoration as I was not there. However, perhaps you may wish to write a letter to the editor of the Regimental Journal and attempt to link up with other members who served with the 5th at that time, or ex officers who might be in a position to say who recommended Sgt. Anderson for his award, and indeed, Sgt. Anderson may well still be alive and could be approached for his version of the story.

Should you still feel that you have been wronged or that Sgt. Anderson was not entitled to the award, I suggest you write direct to the MOD (Ministry of Defence) in London and update them with the information you gave me.

I await the outcome of your quest with interest.

My letter to the MOD:

Ministry of Defence
28th January 2000

My name is John Savage; I was with the 5th Battalion Highland Light Infantry in France on June 8th 1940. I was a member of HQ `C` Company as the CO`s orderly. My army number is 3318052.

Major W. Shaw (Retd) MBE Assistant Regimental Secretary of the Royal Highland Fusiliers suggested that I write to you as you may be able to give me some advice or suggest a course of action for me.

I have attached copies of the letters that I have sent to Major Shaw.

The reply from the MOD is as follows:

17th February 2000
Ministry of Defence

Dear Mr Savage

Thank you for your letter dated 28th January 200 relating to Sgt. Anderson.

We are purely an archive and are not able to comment on the award of the DCM. You may like to contact the following, who may be able to advise you:

MSIB
Metropole Building
Northumberland Avenue
London
* WC2N 5BL*

I am sorry we cannot help you any further with this matter.

Yours sincerely
Mrs S Lawrence
* For Departmental Record Office*

The following letter was sent 22nd February 2000 to the MSIB:

Dear Sir/Madam

The Ministry of Defence Departmental Records Office gave me your address and suggested that I write to you. They feel that you would be able

*to help me with information relating to a Sgt.
Anderson and the award of the DCM he
received.*

*I have enclosed a copy of the letter I sent to the
Ministry of Defence in the hope that you may be
able to help me where they could not.*

Thank you in advance for your assistance.

*Yours sincerely
 Mr J J Savage*

The reply I received from the Ministry of
Defence Dept MSIB Room 341 was from
Lieutenant Colonel R.G. Bird.

Dear Mr Savage

*Thank you for your letter dated 22nd February
2000. It is not possible for us to verify whether
or not Sgt. Anderson has a DCM because you
have not given us his service number or initials.*

*I would point out however, that in order to get a
DCM Sgt. Anderson would not only have had to
be recommended for the award, but his
recommendation would have to have been*

endorsed by a senior committee, both of whom would have taken great care to see that justice was done. I am afraid it is not possible at this late stage to authenticate your version of the event, nor indeed would it be permitted to alter the award of the DCM to Sgt. Anderson.

Yours sincerely
Richard Bird

This next letter is in reply to the above:

Dear Sir
Thank you for your reply to my previous letter. Sgt. W. Anderson's service number is 3313030 and he received the DCM on the 20th December 1940.

I appreciate your comments that his recommendation would have had to be endorsed by a senior committee and that great care would have been taken to see that justice was done. Unfortunately, on this occasion, justice was not done. Somehow the committee have got it wrong. As my previous letter described, I was with Sgt. Anderson and three other men, and that was it; there was nobody else. I lead the Sergeant and three other men to safety.

It was while I was doing some research for my book, some fifty six years after the event that I found out about the award to Sgt. Anderson. I do not know if it is too late, or if it would be permitted to alter an award. I will have to accept your affirmation on that, but because you have been so precise in your reply I feel that at last I am corresponding with someone who will be able to follow this through a bit further for me.

I have written letters to Major W. Shaw (Retd) MBE of the Royal Highland Fusiliers, the Guildhall Library, Aldermanbury, the London Gazette and others. Although they could not help me with any positive information they were kind enough to suggest other addresses I should write to, ending up now with the Ministry of Defence.

My ultimate goal may have been to see the DCM award withdrawn. I do not know, but for now I would like to be able to read for myself the official version of what took place for the award to be recommended and also Sgt. Anderson's account of events. As previously mentioned in my account, the true version of what took place during those days in France is recorded in my book (although never yet published) and is there for anyone to read.

There must somewhere be an official channel open to me to, at the very least, to have my version of events documented and placed along side any other documents relating to the event for future generations to read. Surely it is never too late to hear the truth?

Can you please tell me how I can obtain a copy of the official records relating to what took place for the award to be recommended?
Yours sincerely
Mr J. J. Savage"

The following is the second letter from Lieutenant Colonel R. G. Bird (Retd) and it is dated 17th March 2000

Dear Mr Savage

Thank you for your letter dated 12th March 2000.

Your paragraph two states that "I lead Sgt. Anderson and three others to safety". Sgt. Anderson DCM citation has nothing to do with

leading anyone to safety. He was recommended for carrying a message through to Company HQ by motorcycle under a hail of LMG fire. There is also no "Sgt. Anderson's account of events." Sgt. Anderson, like everyone else, was not allowed to recommend or solicit a recommendation for himself for an award. Indeed the Service have always frowned upon, and actively discouraged, those who seek to promote themselves. You may feel, therefore, that Sgt. Anderson did not deserve an award, but others
disagreed with you and it is entirely wrong to denigrate the award of another man.

My department is the one responsible for honours and awards and if you wish to send in your version of what took place in France, please do so, but not I hasten to add, the whole book.

You may also be interested to know that no retrospective awards can be made. In June 1946 The King, advised by his ministers, ruled that no further awards would be given for services in World War 11 and this remains the case today.

Finally, I can do no better than quote Sir Winston Churchill, who in March 1944 said:

" "The object of giving medals, stars and ribbons is to give pride and pleasure to those who have deserved them. At the same time a distinction is something which everybody does not possess. If all have it, it is of less value. There must, therefore, be heart burnings and disappointments on the border line. A medal glitters, but it also casts a shadow. The task of drawing up regulations for such awards is one which does not admit of a perfect solution. It is not possible to satisfy everybody without running the risk of satisfying nobody. All that is possible is to give the greatest satisfaction to the greatest numbers and to hurt the feelings of the fewest." "

Yours sincerely
Richard Bird

The following is my reply to the above letter from Lieutenant Colonel Bird OBE:

Dear Sir

I have enclosed my version of what took place in France. This is an extract from my book. I have

100

also enclosed a brief summary of what happened to me when I returned from France, as it had previously been suggested to me that I would have known about Sgt. Anderson's award much sooner than a few years ago.

My account of what took place in France is only a small part of my book which was written before I read anything about Sgt. Anderson. It was only when I read George Blake's Mountains and Flood that I was prompted to research further, but there seems to be very little written of what did happen. Even the official versions are no longer available. As I have previously mentioned, it was Dr Diane Henderson, Research Director of The Scot's at War project who suggested that I try and get my account recorded.

If you read my account and what happened to me afterwards, try to imagine the feeling one has, some fifty years later, when they find out that events that took place have been recorded wrongly.

I am someone who fought, witnessed and survived that time in France. Your last letter seemed hard and officious and suggests by using a quotation from Sir Winston Churchill that all I am seeking is another medal for my collection and to suggest that I could denigrate the war record of another man is entirely out of order. If there is any hint that my account of what happened could belittle another individual then that would be because what I have written is a true and accurate account of events and what was previously recorded seems not to be. Any denigration would then be a result of what was inaccurately recorded before.

Thank you for your time and efforts to date and I look forward to your response.

Yours sincerely
Mr J. J. Savage

The following letter will be the third from Lieutenant Colonel R.G. Bird:

2nd April 2000

Dear Mr Savage

Thank you for your letter dated 23rd March 2000 and your version of what took place in France. You also enclosed Sgt. Anderson's citation for his DCM. The citation shows quite clearly that Anderson's DCM was awarded for delivering a message to Co. HQ under fire. The subsequent journey that the five of you made to rejoin your unit is not mentioned in the citation at all. Your quarrel is with the sentence in Mountain and Flood which attributes Anderson's award to both events. Unlike the citation, Mountain and Flood is not the official record and will, therefore, not be kept in the archives. I suggest if you disagree with what is written in Mountain and Flood that you contact the author. I regret there is nothing further that I can add.

Yours sincerely
Richard Bird

My response to Lieutenant Colonel R.G. Bird:

Dear Sir

Thank you for your letter dated 28th March 2000 and your assistance to date. As you are unable to help any further, could you please suggest a name or department within the Ministry of Defence that would be able to assist me further. I appreciate that your interest is in the award of medals, whereas my concern is that

103

the events be recorded correctly. Any award discrepancy is secondary to this as far as I am concerned.

I know that Mountain and Flood is not an official record of what happened and it is not an accurate account either, but neither is the citation. The information the citation gives is wrong and to clarify this I have listed some points which will show why I know this to be so.

- *Sgt. Anderson was heading in the direction of the farmhouse hoping to meet up with any British units in order to take part in the fighting. He did not know about the withdrawal.*

- *Sgt. Anderson had two lads with him. They had been with him for about six hours so he must have met at approximately 15:00 hrs the same afternoon. He was not riding a motorcycle.*

- *The withdrawal orders took place in the evening at approximately 20:00 hr.*

- *The Sgt. did not take part in the withdrawal because he did not know that a withdrawal order had been given.*

- *We were a group of five not six.*

- *I believe Sgt. Anderson when he told me his officer had sent him out on a reconnaissance in order to locate German positions and that is why he was missing; he had got lost.*

• George Blake states in his book Mountain and Flood that the Sgt was unable to take part in the withdrawal. This is because he did not have any knowledge of a withdrawal until I told him about it.

• The citation does not state which Company he saved.

With the lack of any official records other than what I know to be an inaccurate citation, it seems that my version should be given some credence.

Yours sincerely
Mr J. J. Savage

The following letter will be the fourth letter received from Lieutenant Colonel R. Bird OBE:

Dear Mr Savage

Thank you for your letter dated 2nd April 2000. I have nothing to add to my previous correspondence and confirm that the Ministry of Defence will not be taking this matter any further.

Yours sincerely
R. Bird

My reply to the above:

Dear Sir
Thank you for your letter dated 12th April 2000.

Although you have nothing further to add to your previous correspondence I should point out that I did ask, in my previous letters, for some information from the Ministry, which you have failed to respond to.

Since you have confirmed in your last letter that you are replying on behalf of the Ministry of Defence and not just your department, I must assume that the Ministry cannot or will not provide the information I requested.

I do intend to have my account of events printed and recorded and your letters will be part of this, showing the Ministry's reluctance to acknowledge events were, or could have been, different from those previously written.

Sincerely
Mr J. J. Savage.

THE END?

Glenn G. Morrison
1189 Dover Ave.
Columbus, OH. 43212
614-291-8147

Printed in Great Britain
by Amazon.co.uk, Ltd.,
Marston Gate.